Sell Like Never Before

The Ultimate Guide to Skyrocketing Your Sales and Winning Clients

Juliet Bloch

Table of content

Table of content	1
Copyright © 2024 by Juliet Bloch	3
Introduction	4
Chapter 1: Understanding the Psychology of Sales	**10**
The Power Of Persuasion	11
Establishing trust and rapport	14
Overcoming Objections	17
Chapter 2: Making Your Irresistible Offer	**22**
Identifying your unique value proposition	23
Sellable Pricing Strategies	25
Creating Compelling Sales Proposals	28
Chapter 3: Mastering the Art of Communication	**33**
Effective Listening Skills	34
The Art Of Pitching	37
Body language and nonverbal communication	39
Chapter 4: Leveraging Technology for Sales	**43**
Harnessing Social Media for Sales	44
Utilizing CRM Systems Effectively	47
Automation and Scaling Techniques	50

SELL LIKE NEVER BEFORE

Chapter 5: Developing and Nurturing Client Relationships — **55**
   Strategies for Client Acquisition — 56
   Customer Relationship Management — 59
   Retention and Loyalty Programs — 62

Chapter 6: Closing the Deal with Confidence — **66**
   Effective Closing Techniques — 67
   Negotiation Strategies — 70
   Managing Rejections and Obstacles — 72

Chapter 7: Continuous Improvement and Adaptation — **76**
   Tracking and assessing sales performance — 77
   Learn from both achievements and failures — 80
   Remaining Ahead in a Dynamic Market — 83

Conclusion — **88**

SELL LIKE NEVER BEFORE

Copyright © 2024 by Juliet Bloch

All rights reserved. No part of this publication may be reproduced, distributed, or transmitted in any form or by any means, including photocopying, recording, or other electronic or mechanical methods, without the prior written permission of the publisher, except in the case of brief quotations embodied in critical reviews and certain other noncommercial uses permitted by copyright law.

SELL LIKE NEVER BEFORE

Introduction

Mary, a young entrepreneur, once lived in a vibrant metropolis loaded with endless prospects and tough rivalry. Mary had a dream: to develop a prosperous company that would not only support her financially but also have a huge influence on the lives of her clients. However, there remained one huge hurdle standing in her way: sales.

Mary has always been enthusiastic about her goods and services. She put her heart and mind into developing the greatest possible items, but when it came to selling them, she was bewildered. Despite her devotion and hard work, her sales statistics remained flat, and she failed to obtain new customers.

Mary approached a dusty old bookshop situated in a secluded corner of the city one day, feeling indignant and unhappy. Intrigued, she stepped inside, expecting to find some inspiration to feed her business drive. As she scanned the shelves, one specific book grabbed her attention: "Sell Like Never Before : The Ultimate Guide to Skyrocketing Your Sales and Winning Clients."

Curiosity aroused, Mary went for the book and started to flick through its pages. With each chapter she read, she felt a wave of

SELL LIKE NEVER BEFORE

excitement and possibility rise within her. The book claimed to uncover the secrets of outstanding selling, giving practical strategies and proven procedures to aid entrepreneurs like her in attaining amazing sales progress.

Mary, determined to turn her business around, acquired the book and immediately started reading it. The author's tales of victory and reinvention attracted her from the first page. The book emphasizes the power of persuasion, the art of communication, and the value of creating true connections with customers via fascinating anecdotes and real-life scenarios.

SELL LIKE NEVER BEFORE

Mary dug more into the chapters and found several outstanding ideas and realistic recommendations. She learned how to build enticing offers that spoke directly to her target audience, how to successfully explain the value of her goods and services, and how to utilize technology to enhance her sales process.

But, perhaps most crucially, Mary learned the genuine core of selling: it wasn't about pushing items or completing transactions, but about solving issues and supporting people. Armed with this newfound insight, she went on a voyage of self-discovery and growth, pushing herself to move outside of her comfort zone and accept new chances.

SELL LIKE NEVER BEFORE

Mary put the book's teachings into practice daily, and the results were nothing short of remarkable. Her sales soared, her customer base grew, and her company prospered like never before. But, more than financial gain, Mary found delight and satisfaction in knowing that she was having a big effect on the lives of her clients.

As she reflected on her journey, Mary understood that the secret to selling like never before was not simply following a set of tactics or processes, but also creating a mentality of abundance, honesty, and empathy. It was about believing in the worth of her goods and caring about the needs of her clients.

SELL LIKE NEVER BEFORE

So, dear reader, if you find yourself facing similar issues in your firm, remember that you can sell like never before. By implementing the ideas and tactics presented in this book, you, too, can fulfill your full potential, accomplish great sales growth, and win the hearts of your customers. So go with confidence and conviction, and may your path be blessed with success, pleasure, and boundless prospects.

SELL LIKE NEVER BEFORE

Chapter 1: Understanding the Psychology of Sales

Understanding the intricacies of human psychology in sales could be the difference between success and failure. From the time a prospective consumer discovers your product or service until the final decision to purchase, a sophisticated interplay of emotions, justifications, and prejudices unfolds. In this chapter, we will move deeper into the intriguing topic of sales psychology, addressing the power of persuasion, the significance of creating trust and rapport, and successful objection-overcoming tactics.

The Power Of Persuasion

At its foundation, sales is the art of persuasion. It's about influencing someone to take action, whether it's making a purchase, signing up for a service, or getting into a relationship. However, persuasion is more than simply flashy marketing strategies or slick sales speeches; it is about knowing what drives human behavior and applying that knowledge to influence decision-making.

Reciprocity is a very compelling idea. People have an instinctive urge to return minor favors or gestures. Delivering anything of value beforehand, whether it's a free sample, helpful advice, or a customized suggestion, may establish a feeling of duty in the receiver, making them more motivated to reciprocate by making a purchase or executing the requested action.

Another essential idea is social proof. Humans are social animals who frequently seek others for direction on how to act. You may leverage this need for social validation by showing testimonials, reviews, or endorsements from delighted customers, reassuring prospective shoppers that they are making a wise decision in picking your product or service.

Scarcity is another excellent persuasive method. People are naturally attracted to things that are one-of-a-kind or in limited quantity, and they are more driven to act when they fear they may lose out. By stressing the scarcity of your product or service, whether via limited-time discounts, exclusive promotions, or low-stock alerts, you may generate a feeling of urgency that motivates customers to act immediately.

But maybe the most crucial part of persuasion is honesty. Customers in today's hyper-connected world are more informed and discriminating than ever. They can smell insincerity from a mile away and will swiftly disregard anything that sounds manipulative or inauthentic. To properly convince someone, you must first win their trust by being real, honest, and empathic. When people believe you have their best interests at heart, they are significantly more willing to listen to your message and take the proper action.

Establishing trust and rapport

Trust is the cornerstone of all successful sales interactions. Without trust, even the most tempting product or service would struggle to establish momentum in the market. Building trust starts with the first encounter with a prospective client and continues throughout the complete sales process.

Active listening is one of the most effective ways of creating trust. People want to be heard and understood, and by taking the time to listen to their wants, worries, and ambitions, you may display empathy and develop rapport. Ask open-ended questions, seek clarification as required, and show genuine interest in what the other person has to say.

Consistency is another crucial component in developing trust. People are more inclined to trust someone trustworthy, predictable, and consistent in their conduct and words. Make sure you follow through on your pledges, meet your obligations, and maintain a high degree of professionalism at all times.

SELL LIKE NEVER BEFORE

Transparency is also vital in developing confidence. Be upfront and honest about your product or service, including any restrictions, downsides, or possible hazards. Transparency generates authenticity, and when people believe you are being honest with them, they are significantly more willing to trust you and feel secure about doing business with you.

Do not underestimate the role of social evidence in creating trust. Testimonials, reviews, case studies, and endorsements from delighted customers may all assist in convincing prospective consumers that they are making a wise decision by acquiring your product or service. Encourage pleased

SELL LIKE NEVER BEFORE

customers to publicly share their experiences, and be sure to showcase these testimonials prominently on your website, social media platforms, and marketing literature.

Overcoming Objections

Regardless matter how tempting your product or service is, you will likely receive objections from prospective purchasers at some point along the sales process. Objections are a regular element of the purchasing process and may emerge for several reasons, ranging from worries about price or quality to skepticism about the value proposition or appropriateness of the product or service.

The key to overcoming objections is to confront them head-on with empathy and understanding. Rather than rejecting concerns or attempting to argue your way out of them, take the time to listen to the other person's difficulties and validate their viewpoint. Acknowledge their criticisms immediately and honestly, and then work to design a solution that solves their difficulties and satisfies their requirements.

One successful method for overcoming objections is to reframe them as possibilities for further conversation. Instead of perceiving objections as hurdles to a sale, see them as useful input that may help you better understand your customer's expectations and preferences. Ask probing questions to better comprehend the underlying reasons behind the criticism, and then change your answer appropriately.

Another successful way is to present facts and examples that illustrate the value proposition of your product or service. Use case studies, testimonials, statistics, or demonstrations to underline the advantages of selecting your solution over alternatives. When customers see actual proof of the value you can deliver, they are significantly more inclined to overcome their doubts and continue with the purchase.

SELL LIKE NEVER BEFORE

Do not be afraid to ask for the sale. Objections are sometimes used by potential buyers to assess your confidence and conviction in your product or service. By demonstrating confidence in your product and properly explaining the value proposition, you may instill confidence in the consumer and persuade them that they are making the right decision.

Understanding the psychology of sales is critical to success in today's competitive environment. Understanding the fundamentals of persuasion, building trust and rapport, and effectively overcoming hurdles allows you to design a sales process that is not only more productive but also more enjoyable for both you and your customers. So, embrace the power of psychology in your sales plan and watch your business grow like never before.

SELL LIKE NEVER BEFORE

Chapter 2: Making Your Irresistible Offer

In the competitive world of modern business, having an appealing proposal is critical to success. Your offer is more than a product or service; it is a promise, a solution to your consumers' problems, and an expression of your brand's values and identity. In this chapter, we will go over the key components of creating an irresistible offer, such as defining your unique value proposition, pricing strategies that sell, and creating compelling sales proposals that pique your target audience's attention and imagination.

SELL LIKE NEVER BEFORE

Identifying your unique value proposition

Every effective offer is built on a unique value proposition, which is a clear and compelling statement that articulates the benefits and advantages of choosing your product or service over alternatives. Your value proposition is what distinguishes you from the competition and makes your product appealing to your intended audience.

To uncover your value proposition, begin by asking yourself a few key questions:

1. What problem does my product or service solve for my customers?

2. What distinguishes my offer from competing alternatives?

3. What practical benefits or consequences may clients expect from accepting my offer?

4. How does my offer address the needs, ambitions, and preferences of my target audience?

Once you understand the distinct value that your product provides, compress it into a succinct and powerful statement that represents the essence of your offer in a way that resonates with your target audience. Your value offer should be straightforward, concise, and customer-focused, emphasizing the specific benefits and advantages that distinguish your service from rivals.

For example, if you sell productivity software to busy professionals, your value proposition might be something like this: "Streamline your workflow, boost your productivity, and reclaim your time with our intuitive and feature-rich productivity app."

Sellable Pricing Strategies

Pricing is an important aspect of any service, and the right pricing strategy may mean the difference between whether or not your offer is appealing to your target audience. But price is more than just a number; it's about assessing the perceived worth of your product, pricing it right, and effectively communicating that value to your customers.

One common pricing strategy is cost-plus pricing, in which you calculate the cost of producing your product or delivering your service and then add a markup to determine the selling price. While this method is fundamental, it ignores factors such as customer demand, competitor pricing, and the perceived value of your service.

Another strategy is value-based pricing, which involves setting your fees depending on your customers' perceived value of your goods. This strategy allows you to capture more of the value you provide to your customers, which may result in higher profit margins and more customer satisfaction. To implement value-based pricing, you must first understand your consumers' needs, desires, and pain points, and then position your offer as the solution that provides the most value to them.

Alternatively, you may utilize a penetration pricing strategy, in which you set your rates lower than your rivals' prices to quickly attract customers and gain market share. While this strategy may be useful in the short term, it may not be sustainable in the long run, since it may reduce profit margins and create the image of low quality or value.

The ideal pricing strategy for your product will be determined by factors such as your target market, competitive climate, and business objectives. Experiment with various pricing strategies, examine the results and adjust your strategy accordingly to find the price plan that maximizes the perceived worth of your product and increases sales.

Creating Compelling Sales Proposals

A compelling sales proposal is an opportunity to demonstrate the value of your company and motivate potential customers to take action. Whether you're offering a new product to a potential client or presenting a service package to a prospect, your sales proposal should be clear, concise, and persuasive, capturing your audience's attention and imagination from the first page.

Begin by clearly describing the problem or need that your offer addresses, and then position your offer as the solution. Highlight the major benefits and advantages of using your product, focusing on the specific outcomes or achievements that customers may expect to achieve. Use enticing language and images to bring your offer to

SELL LIKE NEVER BEFORE

life, making it genuine and accessible to your target audience.

In addition to emphasizing the benefits of your product, your sales proposal should address any potential objections or concerns that your target audience may have. Anticipate concerns and provide facts, testimonials, or case studies to demonstrate the effectiveness and integrity of your service. Addressing issues early may help you build trust and confidence with your audience, increasing the likelihood of completing the transaction.

Add a call to action encouragi tong your audience to take the next step. Make it easy

SELL LIKE NEVER BEFORE

for potential customers to take advantage of your offer, whether it's scheduling a consultation,
enrolling in a free trial, or making a purchase. Provide clear instructions and contact information, and be willing to follow up with additional information or assistance as needed to enhance the decision-making process.

Crafting an appealing offer involves a thorough knowledge of your target demographic, a clear statement of your unique value proposition, and effective pricing and proposal tactics that convey the worth of your offer and drive prospective buyers to act. By concentrating on these

SELL LIKE NEVER BEFORE

important components, you can design offers that stand out in a congested marketplace and yield sales like never before.

SELL LIKE NEVER BEFORE

Chapter 3: Mastering the Art of Communication

Communication is at the center of any effective interaction, and in the world of sales, understanding the art of communication may be the difference between completing a transaction and losing a prospective client. In this chapter, we will look at three crucial components of successful sales communication: good listening skills, pitching strategies, and the relevance of body language and nonverbal clues.

Effective Listening Skills

Effective listening is the cornerstone of excellent communication. It is not enough to merely hear what your consumers are saying; you must also listen, comprehend, and sympathize with their needs, challenges, and goals. By refining your listening talents, you may create rapport, display empathy, and unearth useful insights that may modify your sales plan and help you better serve your consumers.

One of the keys to successful listening is being present in the moment. Set aside distractions like your phone or computer and offer your complete focus to the person you're conversing with. Maintain eye contact, nod your head, and utilize verbal and nonverbal indicators to convey that you're interested and actively listening to what they're saying.

Another crucial part of successful listening is active listening. This includes not merely listening to what the other person is saying, but also actively interacting with their words, asking clarifying questions, and striving to comprehend their viewpoint. Paraphrase what you've heard to convey your comprehension and respect for their point of view.

Empathy is also needed for successful listening. Consider the other person's viewpoint and attempt to comprehend their emotions, motives, and worries. Empathy may help you create trust and connection with your consumers, making the sales process more fun and productive for both sides.

Be open-minded and responsive to criticism. Listening is more than merely hearing what you want to hear; it's about being open to examining other ideas and opinions, even if they contradict your own beliefs or preconceptions. Being open to criticism helps you to develop as a sales professional while also strengthening your communication abilities continually.

SELL LIKE NEVER BEFORE

The Art Of Pitching

The art of pitching is more than simply presenting a planned sales presentation; it's about personalizing your message to connect with your audience, addressing their individual needs and problems, and compelling them to act. Whether you're selling a product, a service, or an idea, the key to success is to develop a fascinating narrative that piques your audience's attention and imagination.

Understanding your target audience is one of the first stages in crafting a strong pitch. Take the time to investigate your target market, learn about their requirements and interests, and customize your message appropriately. Speak their language, address their pain spots, and position your offer as the answer they have been seeking.

Another key to pitching is to begin with value. Instead of concentrating solely on the features of your product or service, underline the particular advantages and results that clients may anticipate obtaining. Show them how your service can help them simplify their life, save them time and money, or help them reach their objectives.

In addition to leading with value, it is vital to develop credibility and trust with your audience. Provide relevant examples, case studies, or testimonials that show the usage and dependability of your product. By offering proof of your track record and successes, you may improve your audience's confidence and preparation to act.

Do not overlook the power of narrative in your pitch. Humans are predisposed to react to tales, and a well-crafted story can arouse curiosity, provoke emotion, and motivate action. Use tales, analogies, and metaphors to make your message more remembered and effective for your target audience.

Body language and nonverbal communication

In sales, body language and nonverbal communication may expose more than simply your words. Understanding the art of body language enables you to generate trust, establish connections, and create a favorable image with your consumers.

One of the most crucial parts of body language is keeping proper posture and eye contact. Stand or sit up straight, and establish eye contact with the person you're conversing with. This indicates confidence, engagement, and respect, which may assist in developing a feeling of connection and rapport.

Gestures are another key part of body language. Use your hands and arms to underline essential points and bring passion and energy into your speech. Avoid crossing your arms or looking closed off, as these may reflect defensiveness or disinterest.

Facial expressions are equally vital in communicating your emotions and intentions. Smile honestly and utilize facial expressions to show empathy, excitement, and sincerity. Your facial expressions should complement the tone and substance of your message, supporting your verbal communication and magnifying its effect.

Pay attention to the nonverbal indications of your audience. Observe their body language, facial expressions, and gestures to establish their degree of participation and receptivity. To generate a feeling of camaraderie and connection, match your body language to theirs.

The ability to communicate effectively is vital for sales success. By establishing outstanding listening skills, generating engaging pitches, and understanding the intricacies of body language and nonverbal communication, you may generate trust, rapport, and meaningful relationships with your consumers, resulting in greater sales and long-term partnerships. So strengthen your communication abilities and watch your sales fly to new

Chapter 4: Leveraging Technology for Sales

Success In the fast-paced and ever-evolving world of sales, remaining ahead of the curve entails adopting the newest technologies to improve operations, enhance efficiency, and drive revenue growth. In this chapter, we will investigate three important components of employing technology for sales success: using social media for sales, installing customer relationship management (CRM) systems effectively, and embracing automation and scaling ways to maximize efficiency and effectiveness.

Harnessing Social Media for Sales

Social media has revolutionized the way organizations connect with customers, offering a solid platform for boosting brand awareness, driving engagement, and generating leads. By harnessing the power of social media for sales, you can reach a broader audience, develop relationships with potential customers, and drive conversions like never before.

One of the first phases in utilizing social media for sales is to locate the platforms where your target audience spends the most time. Whether it's Facebook, Instagram, LinkedIn, Twitter, or TikTok, recognizing where your audience is engaged may assist you in focusing your efforts and resources more effectively. Once you've picked the right platforms, it's crucial to create a strong and consistent presence by sharing helpful content, communicating with your audience, and compellingly showcasing your goods or services. Use a variety of content types, such as blog posts, videos, images, and infographics, to keep your audience engaged and interested.

In addition to organic content, consider investing in paid advertising on social media to widen your reach and target particular portions of your audience. Social media advertising has extensive targeting options, allowing you to engage people based on demographics, hobbies, habits, and more.

Another productive strategy for employing social media for sales is to engage in social selling, which comprises using social media platforms to discover, connect with, and nurture new prospects. Build relationships with your audience by giving value, making targeted ideas, and engaging in two-way conversations. Don't dismiss the value of analytics and measurement in your social media strategy. Use tools like Facebook Insights, Instagram Insights, and Google Analytics to evaluate crucial metrics such as engagement, reach, conversions, and ROI.

SELL LIKE NEVER BEFORE

By evaluating the data, you can learn what's working, and what's not, and make intelligent decisions to optimize your social media efforts for optimum impact.

Utilizing CRM Systems Effectively

Customer relationship management (CRM) systems are effective tools for maintaining and building customer ties throughout the sales process. By centralizing client data, automating repetitive tasks, and delivering insights into customer behaviour, CRM systems assist sales teams to execute more efficiently and effectively, ultimately producing revenue growth.

One of the key benefits of CRM systems is their ability to concentrate customer data on a single, uniform platform. Instead of fragmented spreadsheets, email inboxes, and paper files, CRM systems provide a single repository for preserving and managing customer information, including contact data, interactions, purchase history, and preferences. By having all this information immediately accessible, sales teams can better understand their customers' needs and preferences, alter their sales presentations and ideas properly, and offer a more tailored and engaging experience.

CRM systems also allow automation of repetitive activities, such as data entry, lead scoring, and follow-up reminders. By automating these arduous activities, sales teams may save time and focus their efforts on other high-value duties, such as developing relationships with prospects and closing agreements.

Furthermore, CRM systems provide crucial insights into customer behaviour and trends, helping sales teams uncover prospects for upselling, cross-selling, and retention. By examining data such as purchase history, browsing behaviour, and engagement indicators, sales teams may anticipate client needs and proactively offer relevant things or services. In addition to internal benefits, CRM systems also improve

SELL LIKE NEVER BEFORE

collaboration and communication across departments. With shared access to customer data and insights, marketing, sales, and customer support teams can coordinate their efforts more effectively, offering a seamless and consistent experience for customers at every touchpoint.

Automation and Scaling Techniques

Automation and scaling techniques are crucial for maximizing efficiency and effectiveness in sales operations, enabling teams to handle greater numbers of leads and prospects without compromising quality or distinctiveness. By automating boring labour, improving processes, and using scalable strategies, sales teams may achieve improved productivity, speedier growth, and better results.

One of the most prevalent uses of automation in sales is lead nurturing. Instead of manually reaching out to each prospect individually, sales teams may leverage email automation systems to offer specialized, targeted messages at scale. By segmenting leads based on demographics, interests, and behaviour, sales teams can personalize their message to the particular needs and preferences of each audience segment, enhancing the chance of engagement and conversion. Another area where automation may be very beneficial is in prospecting and outreach. Instead of spending hours manually hunting for leads and sending cold emails, sales teams may employ prospecting tools and automation technology to locate and reach out to new prospects more rapidly.

By combining data and technology, sales teams may uncover high-quality prospects, adapt their approach, and speed up the prospecting process. Automation may also be utilized for administrative processes such as data entry, scheduling, and reporting. By automating these arduous activities, sales teams may save substantial time and resources, allowing them to focus on more important responsibilities such as developing relationships with prospects, making sales calls, and completing deals.

Furthermore, scaling tactics such as sales funnels and procedures may assist sales teams to manage and prioritize leads more effectively, ensuring that no opportunity gets through the cracks. By mapping out the customer journey from awareness to conversion and beyond, sales teams can establish structured processes and systems for managing leads at each stage of the sales funnel, increasing efficiency and effectiveness.

Leveraging technology for sales success entails a combination of strategy, tools, and techniques. By adopting social media for sales, deploying CRM systems effectively, and applying automation and scaling methodologies, sales teams can simplify processes, enhance productivity, and drive revenue growth like never before.So, embrace the power of technology in your sales approach, and watch your business thrive in the digital era.

SELL LIKE NEVER BEFORE

Chapter 5: Developing and Nurturing Client Relationships

In the area of sales, creating and sustaining customer connections is important to long-term success. Beyond merely closing a transaction, building strong connections with your customers may lead to repeat business, referrals, and, eventually, sustainable development. In this chapter, we will look at three basic areas of creating and sustaining client relationships: client acquisition techniques, customer relationship management, and retention and loyalty programs.

SELL LIKE NEVER BEFORE

Strategies for Client Acquisition

Client acquisition is the process of discovering and recruiting new customers for your firm. While getting new customers is vital for growth, it is equally crucial to concentrate on attracting the appropriate consumers – those who are the greatest match for your goods or services and are likely to become long-term, loyal clients.

One of the most efficient client acquisition tactics is to determine your target market and design your marketing efforts to reach and interact with this group. Invest time and money in market research to understand your target market's wants, preferences, and trouble areas, and then utilize that information to design distinctive marketing campaigns that connect with your audience.

Another powerful customer acquisition method is to harness the power of referrals and word-of-mouth marketing. Encourage pleased clients to recommend their friends, family, and colleagues to your organization by giving incentives or prizes for successful referrals. Consider cooperating with comparable firms or influencers who may help you reach new audiences and grow your reach.

Networking is another fantastic approach to obtaining consumers. Attend industry events, join professional organizations, and engage in online forums where your target audience hangs out. Build connections with prospective clients by delivering value, sharing ideas and experience, and exhibiting your knowledge in your sector.

Don't underestimate the effectiveness of Internet marketing and digital media in customer acquisition. Invest in a decent website, optimize your online presence for search engines, and utilize social media, email marketing, and content marketing to attract and connect with new customers online.

SELL LIKE NEVER BEFORE

Customer Relationship Management

Once you've obtained a new customer, the next stage is to keep and nurture the relationship to guarantee long-term success and happiness. Customer relationship management (CRM) is the process of managing contacts with current and new customers throughout the customer lifecycle, from initial contact to post-sale support and beyond.

One of CRM's primary advantages is its potential to combine customer data and give a full picture of each client's history, preferences, and interactions with your firm. With all of this information easily available, you can create more tailored and targeted experiences for your consumers, improving delight and loyalty.

CRM systems also allow the automation of regular operations and procedures, including sending follow-up emails, arranging appointments, and monitoring interactions. By automating these time-consuming activities, you may be able to concentrate on other vital responsibilities such as communicating with consumers and delivering outstanding service.

CRM solutions may give critical insights and data to help you boost your sales and marketing efforts. By evaluating data such as

SELL LIKE NEVER BEFORE

customer behavior, purchase habits, and engagement indicators, you may find chances for upselling, cross-selling, and retention, enabling you to optimize each client's lifetime value.

Furthermore, CRM systems allow cross-team cooperation and communication, ensuring that everyone in your firm has access to the same information and works together to satisfy your customers' demands. You can give your customers with a smooth and uniform experience at every touchpoint by breaking down barriers and building a collaborative culture.

SELL LIKE NEVER BEFORE

Retention and Loyalty Programs

Retention and loyalty programs are vital for creating long-term connections with your consumers and driving repeat purchases. While recruiting new customers is vital for growth, maintaining current clients is as, if not more, crucial for long-term success.

One of the most successful retention techniques is to give exceptional customer service and support. Be sensitive to your client's wants and anxieties, and go above and beyond to guarantee their contentment with your goods or services. You can enhance client loyalty and promote repeat business by offering a fun and memorable experience.

Another great retention technique is to give rewards and awards for loyalty. Implement a loyalty program to reward consumers for their continuous business, such as discounts, special offers, or exclusive privileges. By promoting repeat purchases, you may encourage clients to return to your company again and again.

Personalization is also vital for retention and loyalty. Use the data and insights from your CRM system to customize your encounters with customers, adapting your message, offers, and suggestions to their requirements and preferences. You may build your connection with your customers and boost their loyalty to your company by

SELL LIKE NEVER BEFORE

proving that you appreciate and cherish their uniqueness.

Furthermore, do not neglect the necessity of getting in contact with your clientele frequently. Keep them updated about new goods, services, or promotions via email marketing, newsletters, or social media. Being top-of-mind enhances the chance of repeat business and recommendations.

Don't forget to request feedback from your clients frequently. Surveys, polls, and reviews may help you learn about your customers' experiences and suggest areas for improvement. By listening to their input and taking action to repair their concerns, you

SELL LIKE NEVER BEFORE

may indicate that you appreciate their views and are devoted to their satisfaction.

Long-term sales success relies on the capacity to create and nurture client connections. By establishing efficient client acquisition, customer relationship management, and retention and loyalty programs, you can develop strong, long-lasting ties with your clients and support your company's long-term success. So invest in your connections, promote client contentment, and watch your company develop with loyal, pleased customers at your side.

SELL LIKE NEVER BEFORE

Chapter 6: Closing the Deal with Confidence

Closing the transaction is the conclusion of all your efforts in the sales process. It's the moment when all of your efforts pay off and you finally seal the sale with your customer. However, sealing the purchase may be one of the most challenging components of selling, requiring confidence, elegance, and the ability to properly overcome objections and arguments. In this chapter, we'll look at three essential parts of completing the transaction with confidence: effective closing skills, negotiating strategies, and coping with rejections and problems.

Effective Closing Techniques

Effective closing strategies are vital for helping your prospects through the concluding phases of the sales process and eventually convincing them to buy. While there are many various closing approaches you may employ, the objective is to select the ideal strategy depending on your prospect's requirements, preferences, and personality.

The assumptive close is a successful closing method in which you presume the prospect has already taken the decision to purchase and only ask for their confirmation. For example, you may say, "So, when would you like to get started?" This strategy works best when you've created trust with the prospect and they're eager to move ahead.

Another powerful strategy is the trial close, which pushes the prospect to make a tiny commitment or choice that takes them closer to making a purchase. For example, you may ask, "Would you choose the standard or premium package?" This strategy makes you examine the prospect's interest and handle any challenges or objections before asking for the final closure.

The urgency closes Is another wonderful way in which you create a feeling of urgency or scarcity to drive the prospect to make a choice soon. For example, you may present a limited-time promotion or highlight that inventory is running short. By establishing a feeling of urgency, you may inspire the prospect to act now rather than later.

The assumptive close is a tactic in which you assume the sale and begin addressing the practicalities of going ahead, such as delivery dates or payment alternatives. By presuming that the prospect has already agreed to purchase, you may skip any lingering objections or hesitations and move directly to the transaction.

SELL LIKE NEVER BEFORE

Negotiation Strategies

Negotiation is a crucial component of the closing process as it enables you to achieve mutually beneficial agreements with your customers and settle the transaction terms. However, bargaining may be challenging, requiring expertise, patience, and the ability to establish common ground with your opponent. Here are some solid negotiation methods that will help you conclude the sale with confidence:

First, perform your task. Before commencing negotiations, examine your prospect's requirements, interests, and financial limits. Understand their aims and objectives so that you may modify your bargaining tactic properly.

Next, create specific goals and outline your bargaining conditions. Determine your targeted goal and the least acceptable conditions you are prepared to endure. This will assist you to remain focused and avoid making judgments that are not in your best interests.

During conversations, concentrate on creating rapport and promoting a collaborative culture. Listen closely to your prospect's worries and objections, and seek for innovative ideas that fulfill their demands while safeguarding your interests.

Be patient and flexible throughout the talk, and be willing to make compromises if necessary. However, avoid giving away too much too quickly, and always be careful of your bottom line.

Don't be scared to walk away if the conditions of the agreement aren't beneficial or if the prospect is unwilling to negotiate in good faith. Stepping away from a situation could sometimes be the greatest decision to safeguard your interests and reputation.

Managing Rejections and Obstacles

Rejections and barriers are a regular part of the sales process, and how you address them may influence whether or not you conclude the deal. Instead of viewing rejections as failures, consider them chances to learn and develop, and utilize them as stepping stones to success.

Anticipating and reacting to issues proactively is a smart technique for handling rejections. Before making your last pitch, examine any issues the prospect may have and prepare solutions or strategies to resolve them. By addressing concerns before they develop, you may display confidence and overcome opposition more effectively.

Another option is to reframe objections as opportunities for greater debate. Instead of perceiving objections as hurdles to the sale, consider them as useful input that may help

SELL LIKE NEVER BEFORE

you better understand your prospect's wants and worries. Ask probing questions to better comprehend the underlying reasons behind the criticism, and then change your answer appropriately.

Persistence is also essential to overcome rejections and hurdles. If your first effort fails, try again. Follow up with the prospect after a rejection, and continue to give value and establish rapport over time. Sometimes it takes numerous conversations before a prospect is ready to make a choice, so don't be disheartened by early failures.

Do not take rejections personally. Remember, sales is a numbers game, and not every prospect will be a suitable match for your product or service. Instead of concentrating on rejections, concentrate on the good parts of your sales efforts and enjoy your victories, no matter how tiny.

Closing a business with confidence involves excellent closing methods, negotiating strategies, and the capacity to accept rejection and hurdles with grace and perseverance. By mastering these abilities and strategies, you may boost your chances of success in the sales process and eventually reach your objectives. So be confident, and diligent, and never give up on finalizing the sale.

SELL LIKE NEVER BEFORE

Chapter 7: Continuous Improvement and Adaptation

In the dynamic and ever-changing world of sales, the capacity to consistently evolve and adapt is vital for sustaining competitiveness and attaining long-term success. In this chapter, we will look at three crucial areas of continuous improvement and adaptation in sales: monitoring and assessing sales performance, learning from successes and mistakes, and keeping ahead in a changing market.

Tracking and assessing sales performance

Monitoring and measuring sales performance is vital for identifying strengths and weaknesses, optimizing procedures, and driving continual progress. By examining key performance indicators (KPIs) and analyzing data, sales teams may receive useful insights into their performance and make educated choices to promote development and success.

One of the first stages in measuring sales success is to define precise and measurable KPIs that fit with your company's goals. These KPIs could include sales revenue, conversion rates, average transaction size, client acquisition cost, and customer lifetime value. By measuring these KPIs over time, you can analyze the efficacy of your sales activities and discover areas for improvement.

Once you've created your KPIs, you should constantly monitor and analyze your sales data to uncover trends, patterns, and opportunities. CRM systems, sales analytics tools, and dashboards may help you track and visualize your sales activity in real-time. This helps you to rapidly identify areas of concern and take remedial action as required.

SELL LIKE NEVER BEFORE

In addition to gathering quantitative data, it's vital to acquire qualitative feedback from your salespeople and consumers. Conduct frequent performance reviews, one-on-one meetings, and customer satisfaction surveys to identify what's working well and where there may be space for improvement. Listening to feedback and implementing it into your sales plan helps you to confront issues ahead of time and drive continual progress.

Don't forget to celebrate your victories and milestones along the road. Recognize and promote top performers, share success stories with the team, and take time to thank your salespeople's hard work and devotion.

SELL LIKE NEVER BEFORE

Building a culture of acknowledgment and celebration may enhance morale, motivation, and engagement, leading to even greater accomplishment in the future.

Learn from both achievements and failures

Sales growth and development involve learning from both triumphs and mistakes. Whether you've just finished a huge transaction or experienced a setback, taking the time to reflect on what went well and what could have been done better may give useful insights that will influence your future actions and choices.

When reflecting on accomplishments, ask yourself what elements led to the beneficial result. Was it good communication, a compelling value offer, great relationship-building abilities, or something else? Identify the essential factors of success and examine how you may repeat them in future sales chances.

Similarly, when reflecting on failures, ask yourself what aspects led to unfavorable results. Was there a lack of preparation, a breakdown in communication, a mismatch with the prospect's requirements, or something else? Be honest with yourself about what went wrong and examine what you can learn from the experience to prevent making the same errors in the future.

In addition to reflecting on individual achievements and failures, it is vital to study wider trends and patterns in your sales performance. Look for common themes or reoccurring difficulties that may be influencing your overall performance, and evaluate what modifications you may take to overcome them. This can entail enhancing your sales process, fine-tuning your presentation, or investing in additional personnel training and development opportunities.

SELL LIKE NEVER BEFORE

Do not hesitate to receive opinions and recommendations from others. Ask coworkers, mentors, or industry experts for input on your performance and development opportunities. By seeking feedback from others, you obtain useful insights and new views that will help you grow and develop as a sales professional.

Remaining Ahead in a Dynamic Market

To remain ahead in a competitive market, you must be adaptable, inventive, and prepared to change. With technology, client habits, and market circumstances continuously evolving, sales teams must be proactive in altering their tactics and techniques to stay relevant and competitive.

One of the keys to keeping ahead in a turbulent market is to be informed and up to speed on industry trends, market changes, and new technology. Make a point of reading business publications, attending conferences and seminars, and networking with other experts in your sector. By being up-to-date on the newest trends and developments, you can predict market changes and modify your plans appropriately.

Accepting innovation and experimentation is another key component of remaining

SELL LIKE NEVER BEFORE

competitive in a changing industry. Don't be hesitant to explore new strategies, test new technology, and seek new markets. Be open to criticism and ready to learn from both triumphs and mistakes and then utilize this information to iterate and improve your approaches over time.

In addition to embracing innovation, your sales technique should stress client-centricity. Focus on knowing your customers' objectives, preferences, and pain spots, and personalize your goods, services, and communications to their individual needs and anxieties. You can separate yourself from the competition and develop long-term connections with your consumers

SELL LIKE NEVER BEFORE

by prioritizing the consumer and giving value at every touchpoint.

Maintain a flexible and diversified approach to sales. Prepare to adjust fast in reaction to market developments, consumer feedback, or competition challenges. By being flexible and responsive, you can boldly grab fresh possibilities and overcome hurdles, ensuring that you remain ahead of the competition in a dynamic and ever-changing market.

Sales success relies on constant development and adaptation. Sales teams may generate growth, innovation, and long-term success by monitoring and

SELL LIKE NEVER BEFORE

reviewing sales performance, learning from successes and mistakes, and keeping ahead of the curve in a changing market. So accept change, be active, and never stop aiming for greatness in all you do.

SELL LIKE NEVER BEFORE

Conclusion

Congratulations! You've finished "Sell Like Never Before: The Ultimate Guide to Skyrocketing Your Sales and Winning Clients." Throughout this thorough book, we've tackled the complexities of the sales process, delving into methods, strategies, and attitudes that will help you enhance your sales game and achieve remarkable success.

As we complete our trip together, let's take a minute to reflect on the important concepts and insights from each chapter, and how they all contribute to your capacity to sell like never before.

In Chapter One, "Understanding the Psychology of Sales," we discussed the power of persuasion, creating trust and rapport, and overcoming hurdles. Understanding the psychological rules that govern human behavior helps you to better connect with your prospects, soothe their anxieties, and eventually steer them toward a purchase choice with confidence and elegance.

Chapter Two, "Making Your Irresistible Offer," showed the necessity of defining our distinct value proposition, pricing tactics that sell, and producing attractive sales proposals. By designing offers that connect with your target audience and demonstrate clear value, you can separate yourself from the competition and position yourself as the obvious option for your clients.

In Chapter Three, "Mastering the Art of Communication," we explored effective listening skills, pitching strategies, and the significance of body language and nonverbal communication. Understanding the intricacies of communication helps you to develop trust, rapport, and real connections with your customers, resulting in greater sales and long-term partnerships.

Chapter Four, "Leveraging Technology for Sales" taught us how to efficiently employ social media, CRM systems, and automation

SELL LIKE NEVER BEFORE

and scaling approaches to boost sales efficiency and effectiveness. Adopting technology and innovation helps you to simplify operations, boost productivity, and drive revenue growth like never before.

In Chapter 5, "Developing and Nurturing Client Relationships," we looked at techniques for client acquisition, customer relationship management, and retention and loyalty programs. By concentrating on developing exceptional, long-term connections with our customers, we can drive repeat business, recommendations, and, eventually, sustainable development for our companies.

SELL LIKE NEVER BEFORE

Chapter Six, "Closing the Deal with Confidence," taught us excellent closing strategies, negotiating approaches, and how to manage rejections and barriers with grace and determination. Mastering the art of closing helps you to confidently clinch the sale and simply take your prospects to a successful finish.

Chapter Seven, "Continuous Improvement and Adaptation," emphasized the importance of monitoring and assessing sales performance, learning from successes and mistakes, and remaining ahead in a changing market. By consistently aiming for development and adaptability, you may remain competitive, inventive, and adaptable in the face of change.

As we end our tour together, remember that selling like never before is about more than simply completing transactions and generating money; it's about delivering value, establishing connections, and positively influencing your customers' lives. By adopting the principles and tactics discussed in this book, you may revolutionize your sales approach, increase your performance, and achieve tremendous success in your sales career.

So, with confidence, passion, and drive, sell like never before. The world is waiting

SELL LIKE NEVER BEFORE

for what you have to give, and with the information and insights learned from this book, you have all you need to succeed. Here is to your continuing development, success, and happiness in the lovely world of sales. Sell on, and may your trip be full of money, pleasure, and unlimited prospects.

SELL LIKE NEVER BEFORE

SELL LIKE NEVER BEFORE

SELL LIKE NEVER BEFORE

SELL LIKE NEVER BEFORE

SELL LIKE NEVER BEFORE

SELL LIKE NEVER BEFORE

www.ingramcontent.com/pod-product-compliance
Lightning Source LLC
Chambersburg PA
CBHW050325230526
45471CB00005B/2361